631ART.COM PRESENTS:

"SPREAD THE AWARENESS"

A COLORING BOOK FOR PROGRESSIVES

BY EDDIE ALFARO

I AM A
SNOWFLAKE
and together
we are an
AVALANCHE
FREE
FO
AL
I.C.E.
POLICY
IS
ROKEN

"Migrants"
Describe
Hunger
and
Solitary
Confinement
at
For Profit
Detention Center
Mistreated

STOP CAREER POLITICIANS
YOUR VOICE YOUR VOTE
SUPPORT
TERM LIMITS

DESPITE HUGE ADVANCEMENTS IN technology & PRODUCTIVITY, millions of AMERICANS ARE WORKING LONGER HOURS FOR LOWER WAGES

THERE IS SOMETHING
PROFOUNDLY wrong
when .01% OWNS
as MUCH wealth AS
the BOTTOM 90%

Get BiG $ money out of politics and RESTORE DEMOCRACY
MONEY OUT VOTERS IN!
DEMOCRACY IS NOT FOR SALE

STOP THE
FEDERAL GOV.
FROM making
A PROFIT ON
STUDENT LOANS

BiGOtS BeGONe!
NO to
SHA
ON
RESISt HAte
NO NAZI
NO KKK
LOVE NOt HAte
STO
RAC
RISe UP FIGHt BACK

MAKE
LOVE NOT
WAR
UNITE
AGAINST
HATE

SMASH FASCISM!
FASCISM!
RISE UP! FIGHT BACK!
RACISM WRONG

EVERY
HUMAN HAS
rights
WE STAND
TOGETHER
JALITY
NO PROFI
OVER
PEOPL
FREE & EQUAL

STAND UP
FOR JUSTICE
Human RiGHts
AND JUST peace
WE DEMAND EQUAL RiGHtS NOW!!
CIVIL RiGHtS equal FREEDOM
HUMAN RiGHtS 4 ALL

WORKER
RIGHTS ARE
HUMAN
rights
RISE UP
WORKERS ARE NOT SLAVES

END
GUN
NO MORE
SILENCE
END GUN
VIOLENCE
NO M
RE
SUPPORT BACKGROUND
CHECKS FOR ALL
GUN SALES

affordable
HOUSING
NOW!
SU
HOUSING
4
ALL
AFFO
HOU
HOMES
PEOPL
PROFI
COMMUNITY
NEED B4
CORPORATE
GREED
NO MORE
RENT INCREASES

SMASH
FASCISM
& BiGOtRY

f
Coca-Cola
Google
Microsoft
amazon.com
Walm
Marlbo
I AM going
TO EAT YOU

PROTECT
THE republic
TIKI
TORCH
LOSERS
FIGHT FASCISM
& NAZISM

#METOO
#IBELIEVEYOU

WOMEN'S RIGHTS are HUMAN RIGHTS

#Metoo
IF·THE· hashtag makes you uncomfortable then·it's WORKING
THIS·EPIDEMIC· ·too·BIG·to· IGNORE; to IMPORTANT O LENCE.

tHE NRA
has invested
MILLIONS OF DOLLARS
to KEEP GUN
LAWS weak and our
children at RISK.

REFORM·OUR
CRIMINAL
JUSTICE·SYSTEM
TO·BE·SAFER·FOR
EVERYONE.
END·THE
WAR·ON
DRUGS.
CLOSE·THE·SCHOOL
TO·PRISON
PIPELINE
END·PRIVATE·PRISON
358012

MANDATE
UNIVERSAL & IMPROVE
BACKGROUND · CHECKS
FOR · FIREARM · PURCHASE
HOW · MANY MORE?
PROtect KIDS · NOt GUNS

IF WAR IS AN INDUSTRY, how can there ever be peace?
The only answer is no way

POVERTY
IN THE USA ALMOST AS BAD AS IN North KOREA
here ARE 5 MILLION IN NORTH KOREA THAT FACE FOOD SHORTAGE, THE SAME NUMBER IN THE USA IS 45 million.

5,000 homeless kids die on the streets every year as a result of assault, illness, or suicide.

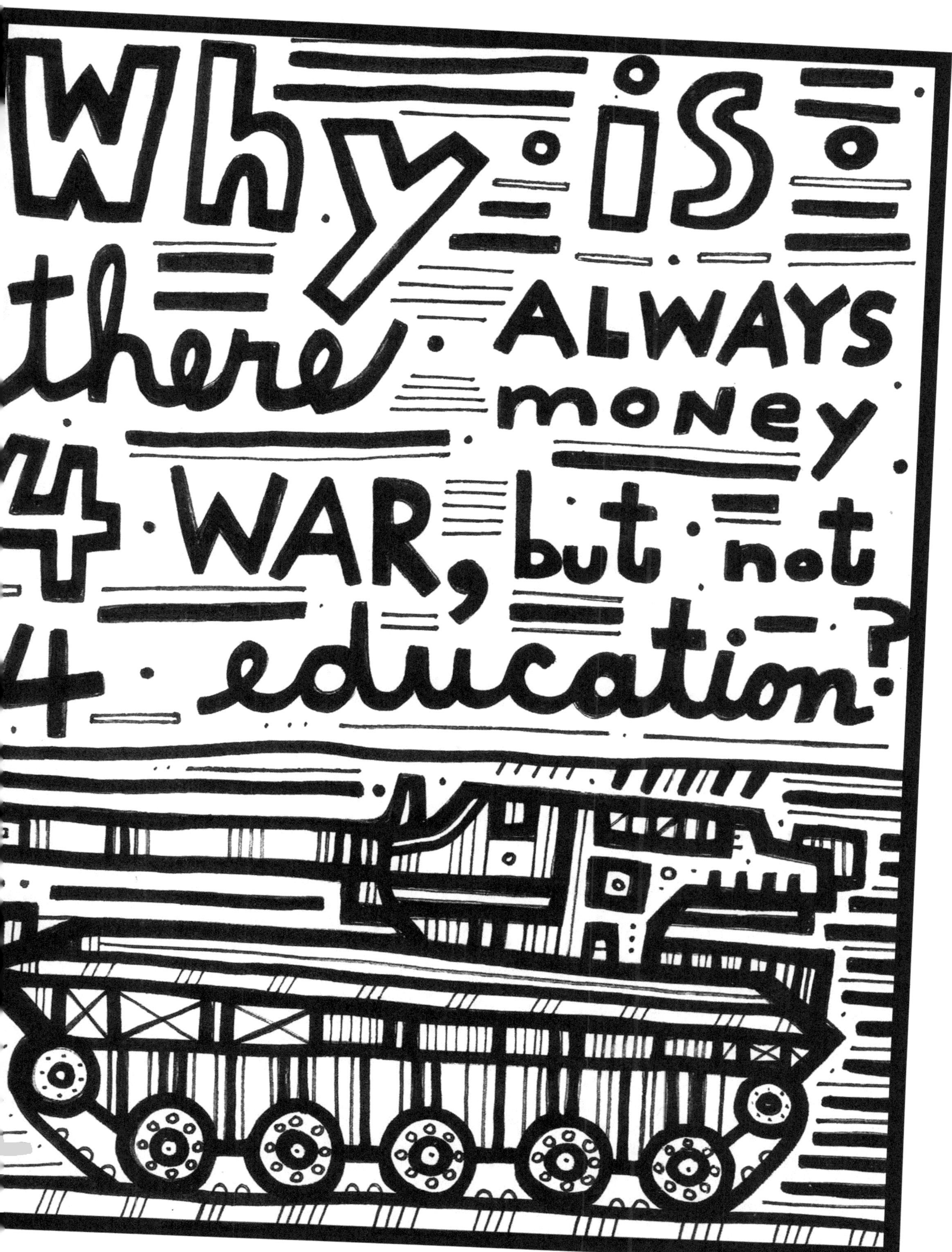

why is there
4 WAR,
4
always money
but not
education?

Every
INDIVIDUAL has the
right to determine the
direction and scope of
his or her FUTURE

EVIDENCE
SUGGESTS THE
MILITARIZATION
OF POLICE FORCES
LEADS TO MORE
CIVILIAN DEATHS

all human BEINGS are BORN FREE and EQUAL IN DiGNitY AND RiGHtS

CLEAN CAMPAIGN FINANCE
BALLOt · BOX
SUPPORt · CANDIDATES
WHO · ReJeCt · LoBBYist
CONtRiBUTiONS

BAN · ALL · BIGOTRY
DEPORT · HATE · SPEECH
BUILD · BRIDGES

A LARGE SHARE OF the WORLD'S wealth NOW RESTS IN THE HANDS OF A SHOCKINGLY SMALL PERCENTAGE OF THE WORLD'S POPULATION
DESPAIR
OST OF THE WORLD'S OUSEHOLDS HOLD HARDLY ANY SSETS AT ALL.

WAGES · IN · THE
U.S.A. have · BEEN
STAGNATING · FOR
THREE · DECADES
YPICAL AMERICAN · WORKERS
ND · LOW · WAGE WORKERS · HAVE ·
EN · NO · GROWTH · IN · REAL WEEKLY WAGES.

UNite!
VICTORY